W9-BEF-212

Official Mensa
Puzzle Book

AWESOME
crosswords

for kids

Trip Payne

Sterling Publishing Co., Inc.
New York

*Dedicated to the National Puzzlers' League, a group that
understands the value of fun and games.*

Other books by Trip Payne:

Crosswords for Kids
Great Crosswords for Kids
Super Crosswords for Kids
Challenging Crosswords for Kids
Clever Crosswords for Kids
365 Celebrity Crypto-Quotes
Mighty Mini Crosswords
Crosswords to Strain Your Brain
The Little Giant Encyclopedia of Word Puzzles (co-author)

Mensa and the distinctive table logo are trademarks of
American Mensa, Ltd. (in the U.S.), British Mensa, Ltd. (in the U.K.),
and Mensa International Limited (in other countries)
and are used by permission.

Mensa as an organization does not express an opinion as being that
of Mensa or have any ideological, philosophical, political or religious
affiliations. Mensa specifically disclaims any responsibility for any
liability, loss or risk, personal or otherwise, which is incurred as a
consequence, directly or indirectly, of the use and application of any of
the contents of this book.

2   4   6   8   10   9   7   5   3   1

Published by Sterling Publishing Co., Inc.
387 Park Avenue South, New York, NY 10016
© 2004 by Trip Payne
Distributed in Canada by Sterling Publishing
C/o Canadian Manda Group, One Atlantic Avenue, Suite 105
Toronto, Ontario, Canada M6K 3E7
Distributed in Great Britain and Europe by Chris Lloyd at Orca Book
Services, Stanley House, Fleets Lane, Poole BH15 3AJ, England
Distributed in Australia by Capricorn Link (Australia) Pty. Ltd.
P.O. Box 704, Windsor, NSW 2756, Australia

*Manufactured in the United States of America
All rights reserved*

Sterling ISBN 1-4027-1038-0

CONTENTS

INTRODUCTION

If you've never done a crossword puzzle before, you might be thinking, "Where do I start?"

Well, you can start at 1-Across, of course. Maybe you know the first word that goes in the puzzle. If so, great! You're on your way to solving the whole thing.

But maybe 1-Across is something you don't know, or maybe there are a few different answers that might fit there. There's no reason not to start at 1-Down instead. Or 15-Across, or 24-Down, or any other place in the puzzle. When you see something you know, write it in, and things should start falling into place from there. And just like before, you're on your way to solving the whole thing.

However you solve them, I hope you have a lot of fun along the way!

—Trip Payne

PUZZLES

1

ACROSS

1 "So what ___ is new?"
5 Exclamation that's similar to "aha!"
8 Stuff you can see in a museum
11 Princess ___ (character in "Star Wars")
12 ___ instant (very quickly): 2 words
13 Sign of the zodiac represented by a lion
14 John or Jane, for example: 2 words
16 Tool used for chopping
17 Talking-___ (scoldings)
18 Boat that goes underwater, for short
20 Gorilla
23 Victories
26 You could lock your valuables in it
29 Certain infielders: 2 words
32 U-___ (moving van company)
33 Sound you could hear in a cavern
34 Find a sum
35 Commercials
37 Pie ___ mode: 2 words
39 Angry

41 Shoddy: Hyphenated
47 A long time ___
48 "I'm so hungry I could ___ horse!": 2 words
49 What Sebastian is, in "The Little Mermaid"
50 Miles ___ hour
51 Everest and McKinley: Abbreviation
52 Plant that can add flavor to food

DOWN

1 Helper for Santa
2 Ring of flowers, in Hawaii
3 Polite thing to call a man
4 Direction where the sun rises
5 Go ___ diet: 2 words
6 "Green Eggs and ___"
7 What you get when you ask for change for a five-dollar bill
8 Its capital is Montgomery
9 Tyrannosaurus ___
10 Tic-tac-___
12 Not outdoors
15 Small city

16 Person who writes rhymes

19 24 hours

20 Frozen water

21 Large

22 Sweepstakes, for example

23 "This ___ man, he played one ..."

24 The past tense of "is"

26 Superman, for example

27 All the actors in a play

29 Vehicles with two wheels

30 Bed sheets

31 High cards

32 The hair around a lion's neck

33 "Earthworm ___" (cartoon series)

34 Stubborn ___ mule: 2 words

35 Parking ___

36 Sprint

37 Thing in the middle of a tennis court

4

ACROSS

1 With 15-Across, light rays emitted from high-tech devices
6 Network that shows "Will & Grace": Abbreviation
9 Slippery fish
12 Fruit that can have a red peel
13 Your and my
14 "Now ___ seen everything!"
15 See 1-Across
16 Smelled
18 Simple beds
20 Word that can go before "control" or "centered"
21 "Beauty and ___ Beast"
23 Use needle and thread
25 A watermelon contains a lot of them
28 Breeze
30 Half of twenty
32 Many: 2 words
33 Soap ___ (kind of TV show)
35 You might ride to school in it
37 Something to play with
38 You hear with them

40 Crunchy Mexican food
42 Doodads
45 What you dry off with, after a bath
48 "___ men are created equal"
49 Sleep for a short time
50 Where a sports event takes place
51 Dessert that has a crust
52 Attempt
53 Acting like a geek

DOWN

1 Where a scientist works
2 Hairy jungle animal
3 Pointy building in Seattle: 2 words
4 Hokey Pokey ___ (popular doll)
5 Takes a break
6 Negative answers
7 Hamburgers and hot dogs go in them
8 Weeps
9 Pointy building in Paris: 2 words
10 Adam's wife, in the Bible

11 Was in front of everyone else

17 Insect that can bother a dog

19 "Ready, ___, go!"

21 "A bird in the hand is worth ___ in the bush"

22 Joint near the middle of the body

24 "Charlotte's ___"

26 Scooby-___

27 Pig pen

29 "Wild horses couldn't ___ it out of me"

31 Almond, for example

34 "You ___ the boss of me!"

36 Name for the Devil

39 "Twinkle, twinkle, little ___ ..."

41 The hard center of a fruit

42 Baby ___ (clothing store for young children)

43 ___ Baba

44 Secret agent

46 Opposite of "beginning"

47 Put down

5

ACROSS

1 Billboards, for example
4 Plate
8 "What time ___?": 2 words
12 Dog's hand
13 Thought
14 The Indianapolis 500 is one
15 You have two of them on your face
17 Word at the end of a prayer
18 Small circle
19 Insect that lives in a hill
20 Toledo is in this state
22 Tell about danger
25 It's near your waist
28 ___ Angeles, California
29 Was concerned
30 New Year's ___ (December 31)
31 What Homer Simpson says when he's upset
32 Middle-___ (not young or old)
33 Sound from a chick
34 Lifesaving technique that lifeguards need to know: Abbreviation
36 Iced ___ (cool drink)

37 Sounds of laughter: 2 words
39 Shape with three sides
44 Does something with
45 Pig's sound
46 Against the ___ (illegal)
47 Present
48 "That's ___ of your business!"
49 Ending for Japan or Vietnam

DOWN

1 Kind of animal Tarzan hung out with
2 When the sun is shining
3 Muppet who cooked food: 2 words
4 Soil
5 What a bride and groom say: 2 words
6 Stitch
7 "Every cloud ___ a silver lining"
8 Country in the Middle East
9 Patriotic Muppet: 3 words
10 ___ cream sundae
11 Card that's not as high as a jack

14

16 With 21-Down, sound of crying
19 Bread ___ butter
20 Like Mother Hubbard
21 See 16-Down
22 What a happy dog's tail will do
23 "___ we there yet?"
24 Bright color
26 "___ got something to tell you"
27 ___ rally (school spirit event)
29 It might be in a garage
33 Ballpoint ___
35 Not the present or future
36 Opposite of "give"
37 Wrap your arms around a person
38 "___ was saying ...": 2 words
39 2000 pounds
40 ___ Grande (river in Texas)
41 Holiday ___ (hotel chain)
42 ___ Vegas, Nevada
43 Lamb's mother

6

ACROSS

1 Part of the mouth
4 Police officer
7 There are 16 of these in a chess set
12 Perform on stage
13 "How ___ you doing?"
14 The name of the Little Mermaid
15 Soft item that can be tossed
17 Friend of Peter Pan
18 "___ be darned!"
19 Noggin
20 Bald ___ (symbol of America)
23 Depressed
24 It lives in a hive
27 Measure of farmland
28 Ball or doll, for example
29 Say "hi" without speaking
30 The Mad Hatter drank it
31 Corn on the ___
32 Round piece of bread with a hole in the middle
33 What you do in order to play the harmonica
35 Frying ___
36 You might put photos or stamps in one
38 Pocketbook

42 "___ the World" (hit song from the 1980s that raised money for Africa): 2 words
43 Item laid by a chicken
44 "___ only as directed" (instruction on medicine)
45 Sides
46 What nodding your head means
47 It follows Friday: Abbreviation

DOWN

1 Place to find test tubes and beakers
2 Cubes you can find in a freezer
3 School organization: Abbreviation
4 Pay-TV
5 Verbal
6 It's used to hold a tent in place
7 Handled roughly
8 Place
9 Someone who talks a lot
10 Homer's neighbor on "The Simpsons"
11 ___ as a fox
16 The longest river in the world

19 You see stacks of it on farms
20 Have lunch
21 Card that can beat a king
22 It contains a lot of different things: 2 words
23 Cry loudly
25 Christmas ___ (December 24)
26 Long, thin fish
28 Drag a car off the side of the road
29 A magician might hold one in his hand
31 "What goes around, ___ around"

32 Short hair over the forehead
34 What a fisherman uses to get a fish's attention
35 Part of a book
36 In ___ of (impressed by)
37 Was at the front of the pack
38 "___ Ya!" (#1 hit by OutKast in 2003)
39 "The Magic School ___" (cartoon show)
40 Happy ___ clam: 2 words
41 "Flattery will ___ you nowhere"

7

ACROSS

1 First ___ (place in the infield)
5 Small hill with a flat top
9 Drink that contains caffeine
12 ___ and crafts
13 Tools that look like large hatchets
14 Meat that comes from a pig
15 Maple or apple, for example
16 You pour it over cereal
17 The first woman, in the Bible
18 Scalding
19 Go out with
20 Small brown bird
21 "Stop, horse!"
23 Beats it
25 "Hold ___ your hats!": 2 words
27 ___ Bell (fast food chain)
28 Get free
30 City in Alaska
32 Walk back and forth
33 Opposite of west
35 Type of tree

37 Long ___ (way back when)
38 "Out of the frying pan, ___ the fire"
39 Bus driver on "The Simpsons"
40 ___ talk (something a coach gives to the team)
41 "Finding ___" (2003 animated movie)
42 ___ light (shiny sign)
43 "___ you kidding?"
44 The Garden of ___ (place in the Bible)
45 Yes ___ (answer choices): 2 words

DOWN

1 Take a ___ (get clean)
2 It's shot from a bow
3 A doctor listens to your heartbeat with it
4 Ending for "Siam"
5 Baby's first word, sometimes
6 Doors that you use to go outside
7 Make a choice
8 Have questions

9 A doctor checks your temperature with it

10 Parts of a roof that hang over the side

11 The last word of a hymn

19 Information for a computer

20 City in Texas

22 "___ upon a time ..."

24 ___ and rave (talk loudly)

26 Unlocked

28 Excited about something that's going to happen

29 Words on the cake in Wonderland: 2 words

31 ___ John (pop singer)

32 One of the Three Bears

34 In the near future

36 Prefix for "rail" or "tone"

38 Ending for "hero"

39 Yoko ___ (singer who was married to John Lennon)

8

ACROSS

1 Experts
5 Sacks
9 Protective covering for a baseball infield
10 Ending for "respect" or "read"
11 What something costs
14 "An apple ___ keeps the doctor away": 2 words
15 ___ around the bush (waste time)
16 "___ of Light" (Madonna song)
17 Bad action, in religion
18 365 days
19 Colorful item that attracts fish to the bait
20 Shrek, for one
22 Keep
24 Has a snack
26 Mailed
27 Forming a question
29 Trips around the track, to a runner
31 Woodwind instrument
32 Spoken
34 Colorful card game
36 Served a meal to

37 Country whose capital is Teheran
38 "___, crackle, pop"
39 State next to Georgia: Abbreviation
40 What a camper sleeps in
41 Unit of measure that a farmer would use
42 Martial ___ (karate, judo, etc.)
43 At that time

DOWN

1 School groups: Abbreviation
2 It plays music
3 Sweet drink: 2 words
4 "Harriet the ___" (book by Louise Fitzhugh)
5 Movie about a pig that wanted to be a sheepdog
6 "Fuzzy Wuzzy was ___": 2 words
7 Gives an angry look
8 "I have my heart ___ on it"
11 Sweet drink: 2 words

Crossword Grid

1	2	3	4		5	6	7	8				
9					10					11	12	13
14					15					16		
17				18					19			
	20		21			22		23				
		24			25		26					
	27					28		29			30	
31					32		33			34		35
36				37					38			
39				40					41			
				42					43			

12 ___ a living (bring home a paycheck)

13 Private ___ (detective)

18 The Abominable Snowman

19 ___ Lang (girlfriend of Superboy)

21 Tool that gathers leaves

23 "___ me about it!"

25 Someone who makes noise while they sleep

27 One of Adam and Eve's sons

28 Ulysses S. ___ (former U.S. president)

30 Catch in a trap

31 One ___ kind (unique): 2 words

33 Aardvarks eat them

35 Not closed

37 "Give ___ rest!": 2 words

38 It comes before Sunday: Abbreviation

9

ACROSS

1 ___ Groening (creator of the Simpsons)
5 The first man, in the Bible
9 Use a shovel
12 "Don't have ___, man!": 2 words
13 The ___ Ranger
14 Ramada ___ (chain of hotels)
15 They can cast spells
17 The Chicago Bulls' group: Abbreviation
18 Sports stadium
19 Tasting like sugar
21 ___ the table (get ready for dinner)
22 Astronaut's group: Abbreviation
26 Solves "2 + 2," for example
27 They can cast spells
29 One of the tokens in Monopoly
32 Thin fog
33 Health resort
36 Black-and-white animal from China
38 Crunchy Mexican foods
40 "Do ___ say!": 2 words
41 They can cast spells

45 "How was ___ know?": 2 words
46 ___ code (part of a phone number)
47 Bet you make at the start of a hand of poker
48 Prefix for "smoking"
49 ___-door neighbor
50 Greatest

DOWN

1 Mothers
2 Without ___ in the world (happy-go-lucky): 2 words
3 Play hard ___: 2 words
4 Identical ___ (lookalike relative)
5 Muhammad ___ (famous boxer)
6 "___ good turn daily" (Boy Scout slogan): 2 words
7 "Pepper ___" (TV cartoon)
8 Filthy place
9 Had a meal
10 Sleeping: 2 words
11 Small, annoying insects
16 "What ___ do to help?": 2 words

20 "Who ___ that masked man?"

23 Cash machine outside a bank: Abbreviation

24 Chemistry or physics: Abbreviation

25 Sounds the doctor tells you to make

27 Marry

28 Ending for "disk" or "major"

29 European country

30 Must: 2 words

31 White pizza topping

33 Make a ___ (throw a tantrum)

34 Places where ships go in and out

35 Something that's useful to have

37 Strong ___ ox: 2 words

39 Someone who lives in the Middle East

42 State north of California: Abbreviation

43 Toy dinosaur in "Toy Story"

44 Grown-up kitten

10

ACROSS

1 The Devil
6 Columbus Day's month: Abbreviation
9 "Now I understand!"
12 "___ in Wonderland"
13 Long-lasting card game
14 Very heavy weight
15 Capital of Tennessee
17 Didn't follow
18 Electric ___ (kind of fish)
19 Papa's wife
21 "Open 9 ___ 5" (sign on a store window)
24 Went faster than walking
26 Boy Scouts sometimes sleep in them
29 Fix a magazine story
31 "Are we having fun ___?"
33 Spin like ___: 2 words
34 Things you aren't supposed to do: Hyphenated
36 What a spider spins
38 One of the girls in "Little Women"
39 Somewhat cold
41 ___ and reel (fishing gear)
43 ___ Schwarz (toy store)
45 Capital of Iowa: 2 words
50 "___ tell you what ..."
51 How old a person is
52 Smell
53 ___ Affleck (famous actor)
54 The Boston Red ___ (baseball team)
55 ___ bear (stuffed animal)

DOWN

1 ___ Diego, California
2 State next to Mississippi: Abbreviation
3 "My country ___ of thee ..."
4 Pain
5 At no time
6 Bird that hoots
7 The ___ before the storm
8 "Trick or ___!" (Halloween saying)
9 Capital of Georgia
10 Tool used by a gardener
11 Macaroni ___ cheese
16 "Now ___ me down to sleep ...": 2 words

20 "Give ___ break!": 2 words

21 Seven plus three

22 Wedding phrase: 2 words

23 Capital of Nebraska

25 ___ Jersey

27 Cat who chased Jerry in cartoons

28 I ___ (game of observation)

30 Also

32 ___ of endearment (word like "honey" or "sweetie")

35 Soft drinks

37 Help to go higher

40 Brand of toy that you build things with

42 You need five of them to play Yahtzee

43 Small lie

44 Ginger ___ (kind of drink)

46 Gender

47 Mr. Flanders, on "The Simpsons"

48 Dead-___ street

49 Where a pig lives

11

ACROSS

1 Clubs, diamonds, hearts, or spades
5 Used to be
8 Word that can go before "tub" or "robe"
12 Hold ___ (grasp): 2 words
13 Grampa Simpson's first name
14 Where Russia and China are
15 Pro basketball team: 2 words
18 "For crying ___ loud!"
19 What a beaver builds
20 You go under it when you're doing the limbo
23 Color on the American flag
25 Station ___ (kind of car)
29 Its capital is Baghdad
31 Part of a lower-case letter I
33 "That's ___ of your business!"
34 Leave the bed: 2 words
36 It's inside a balloon
38 Father
39 State-of-the-___ (high-tech)
41 West Coast state: Abbreviation
43 Pro basketball team: 3 words

50 "Money is the root of all ___"
51 Slippery sea creature
52 Canvas thing on a boat
53 Boy's name that sounds the same as the girl's name "Jean"
54 Where the pupil and retina are
55 Raggedy ___ (boy doll)

DOWN

1 Weep loudly
2 Card game that has Skip and Reverse cards
3 "___ a small world after all"
4 Dorothy's dog in "The Wizard of Oz"
5 Desired
6 The first three letters
7 It can grow into a plant
8 Bruce Wayne's secret identity
9 "It's just ___ thought!": 2 words
10 ___-tac-toe
11 Possesses
16 "Days of ___ Lives" (soap opera)
17 The ___ of gravity (scientific rule)

20 Huge

21 "You ___ here" (words on a mall map)

22 Animal similar to a mouse

24 ___ good deed (be helpful): 2 words

26 "In ___ we trust" (phrase on U.S. money)

27 "Humpty Dumpty sat ___ wall": 2 words

28 Rod and Todd Flanders' dad, on "The Simpsons"

30 Dan ___ (vice president from 1989 to 1993)

32 ___ Me Elmo (popular doll)

35 Athlete who isn't an amateur

37 Moved really fast

40 Plant in an orchard

42 Mona ___ (famous painting)

43 Opposite of positive: Abbreviation

44 She lived in the Garden of Eden

45 Finish in first place

46 Door opener

47 "You ___ say that again!"

48 Baby goat

49 Sneaky, like a fox

12

ACROSS

1 Toys that go around and around
5 "What a good boy ___!" (what Little Jack Horner said): 2 words
8 Letters after G
11 "I've got a bright ___"
12 Piece of paper taken to the supermarket
14 America: Abbreviation
15 Duplicate
16 "This ___ sudden!": 2 words
17 Frilly white fabric
19 Enjoy a book
21 Take someone to court
22 Joints at the bottom of legs
24 Sewed the bottom of a pair of pants
26 Cast a spell on
27 Cindy-___ Who (character who meets the Grinch)
28 Munches
31 How a preacher would describe bad actions
34 "___ the fields we go ..." (line from "Jingle Bells")

35 "That hurts!"
37 Large, bushy hairdo
38 Went below the water
40 Al ___ (Clinton's vice president)
42 Alter ___ (secret identity)
43 Many people decorate one for Christmas
44 Orangutans
45 Normal number of fingers
46 Make an effort
47 Cincinnati ___ (baseball team)

DOWN

1 ___ Tacs (little breath mints)
2 Bad smells
3 ___ Le Pew
4 What a doctor might tell you to do when he looks into your throat: 2 words
5 "Prince ___" (song in "Aladdin")
6 "Little" girl in a nursery rhyme: 2 words

7 Single copy of a magazine

8 Hawaiian dance

9 "This ___ outrage!": 2 words

10 "Little" boy in a nursery rhyme: 2 words

13 Pigeon-___ (having feet that point inward)

18 School for grades 1 through 5: Abbreviation

20 Sandwich shop

23 Baseball player from Montreal

25 "___ Lisa" (famous painting by Leonardo da Vinci)

28 Price

29 Valentine's shape

30 "___ and spice and everything nice"

31 Tear into tiny pieces

32 Encourage

33 Crazy as a ___

36 Deal with

39 Lock opener

41 Ending for "host" or "lion"

13

ACROSS

1 Short word for what goes into weapons
5 ___ office (place to mail letters)
9 Not high
12 Grizzly ___
13 Car
14 "Four-and-twenty blackbirds baked ___ pie": 2 words
15 Nickname for Batman: 2 words
18 Tree that has acorns
19 Sleep for an hour or so
20 "Every dog ___ his day"
23 Guys
25 It makes bread rise
29 "That's just the way ___": 2 words
31 Letters between C and G
33 Sneaker, for example
34 Where Houston is
36 "___ la la" (sounds in a song)
38 Tool used for chopping
39 "___ the Great Pumpkin, Charlie Brown"
41 State that borders Tennessee: Abbreviation
43 Nickname for Batman and Robin: 3 words

50 "Where there's a will, there's a ___"
51 Opposite of hate
52 ___ Turner (famous rock singer)
53 What the O stands for in "I.O.U."
54 Female animals that have wool
55 "X marks the ___"

DOWN

1 Rival network of CBS: Abbreviation
2 "Oh, give ___ home where the buffalo roam ...": 2 words
3 It shows you how to get from one place to another
4 Black-and-white cookie
5 Filled a suitcase
6 Belonging to the two of us
7 Really surprise
8 "___ the least": 2 words
9 Top of a jar
10 Number of horns on a unicorn
11 Armed conflict
16 It blocks the water in a river

17 "Planet of the ___"
20 ___ the road (leave)
21 Had breakfast
22 Three plus three
24 You could catch butterflies in it
26 Exclamation that reads the same forward and backward
27 The Chicago White ___ (baseball team)
28 Peg used by a golfer
30 Uttered
32 They hold paintings
35 Out of ___ (no longer popular)

37 "___ Baba and the Forty Thieves"
40 Winter weather
42 Plays a part in a movie
43 Number of singers in a duet
44 Hee-___ (donkey's sound)
45 Keep an ___ on (watch)
46 Oriental ___ (space in Monopoly): Abbreviation
47 Short swim
48 Game with Wild and Draw Two cards
49 Kind of grain

14

ACROSS

1 Animals that are very similar to rabbits
6 It may be served with chips
9 "Now I get it!"
12 Grown-up
13 ___ Today (popular newspaper)
14 Brother's sibling, for short
15 Sloppy
16 Language spoken in London
18 Opposite of buy
20 A golf ball could rest on top of it
21 Muhammad ___
23 It might be pierced
25 Mixes together
29 Word after "sun" or "laser"
31 Show ___ (the world of entertainment)
33 Word on an eight-sided street sign
34 Ice cream holders
36 One of the Seven Dwarfs
38 One ___ time: 2 words
39 Tuscaloosa is a city in this state: Abbreviation
41 Spoken, not written

43 Language spoken in Madrid
47 Doors that aren't entrances
50 What painters make
51 Lemon meringue ___
52 It grows in a garden
53 ___ Hanks (famous actor)
54 "What did you ___?" ("I couldn't hear you")
55 Shelters used by campers

DOWN

1 Red meat
2 Ending for "lemon" or "Gator"
3 Language spoken in Moscow
4 "What ___ is new?"
5 In ___ (currently popular)
6 Past ___ (late, at the library)
7 "Money ___ everything!"
8 You turn them in a book
9 "Just ___ suspected!": 2 words
10 Not hers
11 What's left after something is burned

17 Allows
19 Room where people do science experiments
21 Easy as ___
22 A sign of the zodiac
24 Get ___ of (eliminate)
26 Language spoken in Rome
27 Decay
28 Health ___ (place where people try to get in shape)
30 Like a bully
32 Place to see animals in cages

35 Stumbles
37 Moved slowly and sneakily
40 Where India is
42 Rod that's attached to a car's wheels
43 Stopped standing up
44 Full-time athlete
45 Machine that dispenses money: Abbreviation
46 "___, wait a minute!"
48 It's used to blow things up: Abbreviation
49 Cars drive on them: Abbreviation

15

ACROSS

1 Group that sends up space shuttles: Abbreviation
5 The first four letters
9 ___ gun (toy weapon)
12 On ___ with (equal to)
13 Truth or ___ (game)
14 "Do ___ tell you!": 2 words
15 It could cause you to get sick
16 Dish that includes meat and potatoes
17 Use your tongue
19 White spread that's put on sandwiches, for short
21 Golfer's peg
22 Queen ___ (famous rapper and actress)
24 ___ Way (galaxy that the Earth is in)
26 Get wrinkles out of clothes
27 It's produced by a lit match
28 It's produced by a lit match
30 They make paintings and sculptures
33 One of the Bobbsey Twins
34 Farm building that holds grain
36 "Scat!"
37 ___ hygiene (brushing one's teeth)
39 Extra large or small, for example
41 "... and a partridge ___ pear tree": 2 words
42 Barbed ___ fence
43 "And they lived happily ___ after"
44 Pay-___-view (kind of TV show)
45 Toy made by Duncan: Hyphenated
46 "___, meeny, miney, mo"

DOWN

1 Worthless horse
2 "Tarzan the ___": 2 words
3 ___ Michelle Gellar ("Scooby-Doo" actress)
4 Military group
5 They try to sell things
6 Game where you try to sink your opponent's fleet
7 Small river

8 One of Donald Duck's nephews

9 Use the telephone

10 Where Japan and China are

11 Game where you try to draw things

18 Captain in the original "Star Trek"

20 Leave out

23 Enemies

25 A flower, or a part of the eye

27 Like ice cubes

28 Like hills that you can ski down

29 Super ___ Bros. (video game heroes)

30 Not dead

31 Dial ___ (sound on the telephone)

32 Fly high

35 "___ what you mean": 2 words

38 Summertime zodiac sign

40 Ending for mock or trick

16

ACROSS

1 Talks on and on
5 Throw
9 Busy as ___: 2 words
10 Burst ___ flames
11 Garfield, for example
14 Thaw
15 Grouchy
16 ___ conditioning
17 Long, thin fish
18 It could be true-false or multiple-choice
19 Raggedy ___ (male doll)
20 Uses a keyboard
22 Deserves
24 "So ___, so good"
25 Name for a lion
26 Go up a ladder
28 Words that aren't used in proper English
30 Revolving ___
31 Is in a play
33 ___ Franklin (early American inventor)
35 Bratty kid
36 Have a sore muscle
37 Candy ___ (Christmas treat)
38 ___ Moines, Iowa
39 You wash with it in the bathtub
40 "I cannot tell ___": 2 words
41 Six-legged pests
42 Needed a bandage, maybe

DOWN

1 Scrabble is one
2 Red as ___: 2 words
3 Noisy dives into a pool: 2 words
4 ___ a good example
5 The New York ___ (famous newspaper)
6 White dollar bills, in Monopoly
7 Ohio or Oregon, for example
8 Male child
11 Noisy dive into a pool
12 Band-___ (scrape coverings)
13 "___ it, you'll like it!"

18 ___ of endearment (nickname for a loved one)
19 Location
21 Two of a kind, in poker
23 "___ well that ends well"
26 "Easy ___, easy go"
27 Breakfast food
28 Parts of a staircase

29 Robin Williams played one in "Aladdin"
30 "Why ___ the chicken cross the road?"
32 Have a conversation
34 "A friend in ___ is a friend indeed"
36 Light ___ feather: 2 words
37 Taxi

17

ACROSS

1 The last month of the year: Abbreviation
4 Thomas Edison's middle name
8 "As I was going to St. Ives, I met ___ with seven wives": 2 words
12 Ooh and ___
13 Hawaiian rings of flowers
14 Batman wears one
15 Prefix for cycle or angle
16 Knocked for a ___ (really surprised)
17 Use a computer keyboard
18 Luthor, to Superman
20 Mouth part
22 "___ MacDonald had a farm ..."
23 Not out, in baseball
24 Uncommon
25 Author of the Curious George books
26 A surfboard rides on top of one
28 Country near Saudi Arabia
30 Boxer Muhammad ___
32 Word at the end of a prayer
34 Ships that have periscopes

37 Jet ___ (problem for a traveler)
38 Word that goes after "neither"
39 Dish with meat and beans
40 Pulls hard
42 Flowers might be put in it
44 One of Jo's sisters in "Little Women"
45 Stuck in ___ (always doing the same thing): 2 words
46 Network that focuses on sports: Abbreviation
47 Big ___ (famous landmark in London)
48 NFL team from St. Louis
49 Chair
50 A football field is measured in these units: Abbreviation

DOWN

1 Goes to dinner and a movie with
2 ___ living (work): 2 words
3 Police officer on "The Simpsons": 2 words
4 Person who's on the same side as you

5 Zodiac sign that comes before Virgo
6 Stringed instrument
7 Pill that can help a headache
8 "___ your age!"
9 Government official on "The Simpsons": 2 words
10 Crunchy fruit
11 Poor
19 "Give ___ little credit!": 2 words
21 Miles ___ gallon (what MPG stands for)
24 Eliminates
27 Moving truck

29 ___ Wednesday (time before Easter)
30 Place in a church where people get married
31 Wife of George W. Bush
33 Get rid of pencil marks
35 What you might do if a thorn pricks your finger
36 "Yield" and "Don't Walk," for example
39 Word that appears on a penny
41 Roads and avenues: Abbreviation
43 Place where some people go to lose weight

18

ACROSS

1 ___ Ryan (famous actress)
4 ___ in the neck (pest)
8 "___ sesame!" (magic words)
12 In this day and ___ (currently)
13 Hang ___ (keep)
14 Item in a forest
15 High-tech device
17 What a pinball machine says if you shake it too much
18 "Roses ___ red ..."
19 Daughter's sibling
20 Soldiers serve in it
23 Short letter
26 Money that's left for the waiter
29 Ghostly sound
30 Country in Asia
31 The night before a holiday
32 Pro and ___ (sides in a debate)
33 Created
34 Region
35 "This ___ job for Superman!": 2 words
37 Make a hole in the ground
39 Not early

41 It's used with a 15-Across
46 "Thanks ___!": 2 words
47 "___ no reason why not": 2 words
48 "See you later!"
49 Big battles
50 Quiz
51 Make clothing

DOWN

1 Big ___ (kind of hamburger)
2 A conceited person has a big one
3 Jewel
4 Serve liquid from a pitcher
5 Part of a radio or a Martian
6 Ending for "meteor"
7 Neither this ___ that
8 Boy's name that reads the same forward and backward
9 It's used with a 15-Across
10 Fish that's hard to catch
11 It's used to catch fish
16 Spend money

19 Caribbean ___ (big body of water)

20 One of the main TV networks: Abbreviation

21 Kanga's child, in "Winnie-the-Pooh"

22 It's used with a 15-Across

24 Like the numbers 7 and 9

25 Makes colorful clothing, in a way: Hyphenated

27 "___ had enough!"

28 Small green vegetable

30 "___ little teapot ...": 2 words

34 Many years ___ (in the past)

36 Collections

38 "Yeah, sure!": 2 words

39 ___ and order (what the police try to preserve)

40 Apple pie ___ mode: 2 words

41 First-aid ___

42 Ending for "Japan"

43 Muscles that are improved by sit-ups

44 Dark brown bread

45 Moisture that appears on grass

19

ACROSS

1 For the most ___ (mostly)
5 Con game
9 Not many
12 Neighbor of Europe
13 Coca-___
14 How a sailor would say "yes"
15 Major tennis event
17 Color of a strawberry
18 The planets revolve around it
19 The Atlanta Braves, for example
21 That woman
24 "___ for 'apple'": 2 words
26 Kind of fruit
29 Major horse racing event: 2 words
33 Go ___ detail (explain fully)
34 ___-Hoo (brand of chocolate beverage)
35 "Monkey ___, monkey do"
36 Reason for an umbrella
39 ___ favor (help someone out): 2 words
41 "What ___ supposed to say?": 2 words
43 Major football event: 2 words
48 Female deer
49 "American ___" (show that features young singers)
50 ___ code (first part of a phone number)
51 Letters that are a cry for help
52 "That's ___ to me" ("I didn't know that")
53 Wooden items used in golf

DOWN

1 Dog's foot
2 "___ was going to St. Ives ...": 2 words
3 It surrounds a basketball net
4 Keep ___ on (watch carefully)
5 Like a good view
6 Kind of fish
7 Tons: 2 words
8 Horse's hair
9 They work in agriculture
10 The calm center of a hurricane
11 Tuesday follower: Abbreviation
16 Big feast in Hawaii

20 Large jungle animal
21 Piece of winter sports equipment
22 Female chicken
23 Pages of writing in a diary, for example
25 Where the moon is
27 Honest ___ (Lincoln's nickname)
28 Kind of bread
30 "Only one ___ customer": 2 words
31 Sings like Heidi
32 It might have a knob and a bell

37 "The doctor ___" (Lucy's sign, in "Peanuts"): 2 words
38 Naked
40 Blind as ___: 2 words
41 They interrupt TV shows
42 Sound you might hear in a dairy
44 Noise of a punch
45 Metal that's just been mined
46 ___ Willie Winkie
47 ___ Vegas (city in Nevada)

20

ACROSS

1 Wet dirt
4 Animal similar to a frog
8 ___ Lane (girlfriend of Superman)
12 Hard ___ rock: 2 words
13 "At ___" ("Relax," in the military)
14 Cost an arm ___ leg: 2 words
15 Wooden thing that helps keep a tent in place
16 It might be washed up on the beach
18 Gets married to
20 Ending for "north" or "south"
21 Extreme suffering
23 Opposite of night
24 ___ away (escaped)
27 Little Red Riding ___
28 "Ready or ___, here I come!"
29 Nothing
30 Find a total
31 Bar owner on "The Simpsons"
32 Made a secret message
33 Have an ___ for music (be musically talented)
34 What a cat says
35 Where many movies come from

39 Word on a light switch
42 Part of the eye
43 ___ Sewell (author of "Black Beauty")
44 Grease
45 ___ Sampras (famous tennis player)
46 Twelve months
47 Not moist

DOWN

1 It shows you how to get from one place to another
2 "Oh, what's the ___?" ("What difference will it make?")
3 He's married to Blondie, in the comics
4 ___ bear (kind of stuffed animal)
5 Boat paddles
6 "___ was saying ...": 2 words
7 Loss
8 It needs to be mowed regularly
9 Yoko ___ (famous singer)
10 "___ not like green eggs and ham!": 2 words
11 Disappointed

17 Do one's best

19 From beginning to ___

21 "I have an idea!"

22 Zeus was one for the ancient Greeks

23 "___, a deer, a female deer ..."

24 Very large tree

25 "You ___ what you eat"

26 Show agreement

28 Country that's next to Sweden

29 Petting ___ (where you can see tame animals)

31 The month before June

32 Kind of tree that smells nice

33 "What ___ can I say?"

34 "___ Lisa" (painting of a woman with a famous smile)

35 Word you might say twice before "hooray!"

36 State next to Washington: Abbreviation

37 Started a fire

38 "___ of these days ..."

40 Tree that's sometimes used as a Christmas tree

41 Ride in an airplane

21

ACROSS

1 Animal that lives in a cave
4 Water that can be found on grass
7 Casts a ballot
12 Prince who Aladdin pretended to be, in the movie
13 ___ jiffy (quickly): 2 words
14 Have the same opinion
15 Certain nuts
17 Male duck
18 Nights before holidays, like Christmas
19 "Where have you ___?"
20 ___ and dangerous (description of some criminals)
22 ___ Majesty (how people refer to a queen)
23 "___ sells seashells down by the seashore" (tongue twister)
26 Lion's noise
27 Little ___ (small amount)
28 Bigger relatives of monkeys
29 "And on and on": Abbreviation
30 ___ station (place to get fuel)
31 Opposite of back
32 60 minutes
34 ___ pressure (when friends try to force you to do something)
35 Still breathing
37 Candy spills out of them when they're broken
40 18 is equal to two of them
41 "Monsters, ___"
42 A modest person has a small one
43 People older than 12 but younger than 20
44 "Golly!"
45 Straight line

DOWN

1 Sound from a sheep
2 Everything
3 Device in a science fiction story: 2 words
4 Had a nice meal
5 Go to the ___ of the earth
6 "Fuzzy Wuzzy ___ a bear"
7 Darth ___ ("Star Wars" villain)
8 Relative of a troll

9 Device in a science fiction story

10 "Oh no, a mouse!"

11 Use your eyes

16 "___ my dead body!"

19 Gamble

20 "Your eyes ___ bigger than your stomach"

21 Turn bad

22 That guy's

24 Animal that lays eggs

25 Word ending that means "most"

27 Candy ___ (sweet treat)

28 ___ code

30 "I ___ so" ("That's probably right")

31 It may be made of barbed wire

33 What Hansel and Gretel pushed the witch into

34 Kind of tree

35 Fire ___ (insect that stings)

36 "Let sleeping dogs ___"

37 Where bacon comes from

38 "A long time ___, in a galaxy far, far away ..."

39 Boar's wife

ACROSS

1 Defeat
5 Boat's paddle
8 What lips might do in winter
12 It might go before "mobile" or "biography"
13 Boston cream ___
14 Sister of Bart and Maggie
15 Teddy bear, for example: 2 words
18 Gray metal
19 Take a small drink
20 Metal fastening
23 Burst a balloon
24 "You asked ___ it!"
27 Kitchen appliance
28 One plus two plus three plus four
29 Ice cream ___
30 Covered with water
31 Use a ray gun
32 What you'll do if your skin gets cut
33 Very heavy weight
34 Zodiac sign that comes after Cancer
35 G.I. Joe and others: 2 words
42 You hit it with a hammer

43 "A Nightmare on ___ Street" (famous horror movie)
44 Finished
45 Cedar or cypress, for example
46 It's used to color Easter eggs
47 Luke's teacher in the "Star Wars" films

DOWN

1 ___ Vegas (Nevada city)
2 "Get ___ of here!"
3 Letters between R and V
4 Make less hard
5 Not closed
6 Kool-___ (fruity drink)
7 Listen to ___ (do what's sensible)
8 Paper ___ (fastener)
9 That guy
10 Dead ___ doornail: 2 words
11 Good friend
16 Physically ___ (in shape)
17 Small bite
20 "... and pretty maids all in a ___"
21 "___ never been so insulted in all my life!"

22 Animal doctor, for short

23 Word before "talk" or "squad"

24 Enemy

25 "It's just ___ of those things"

26 Color of a cherry

28 Turned one's skin brown

29 Like the sky, when you can't see the sun

31 Where you can visit animals

32 Command to a dog

33 Square piece with a letter on it, in the game Scrabble

34 Jell-O flavor

35 An exterminator might kill it

36 Means of transportation

37 Equal score for both teams

38 Ride in an airplane

39 Kanga's kid, in "Winnie-the-Pooh"

40 Tight ___ (position in football)

41 The Mediterranean ___

23

ACROSS

1 ___ vu (the feeling you've done something before)
5 "As a matter of ___ ..."
9 It's needed to play a violin
12 Slippery ___ eel: 2 words
13 Its capital is Salt Lake City
14 Go ___ wild-goose chase: 2 words
15 Result of a small car accident
16 When Election Day is
18 Make ___ of (put to work)
20 Hole in a needle
21 Country that got its independence in 1776: Abbreviation
23 ___ and Eve
26 ___ a bath (washed)
30 What the P stands for in MPH
31 Fairy ___ (certain stories)
33 Pool player's stick
34 Simon ___ (game)
36 Pull
37 Do what one can
38 Abbreviation after some business names
40 "What did ___ to deserve this?": 2 words
42 When Groundhog Day is
47 "___ to leap tall buildings in a single bound" (Superman description)

50 The Ice ___ (when glaciers covered the Earth)
51 Not false
52 Wooden pegs that golf balls rest on
53 "That's ___ my problem"
54 ___ the table (gets ready for dinner)
55 Music, dance, painting, etc.

DOWN

1 Mom and ___
2 Ending for "Vietnam"
3 When Martin Luther King Day is
4 Have ___ in your pants (be impatient)
5 ___ and games
6 From ___ Z (completely): 2 words
7 People who lived a long, long time ago
8 Those people
9 ___ for apples (play a Halloween game)
10 Kill two birds with ___ stone
11 Card game that takes a long time
17 "You've ___ your match!"

19 Have a snack
21 ___ and downs
22 Word before "horse" or "shell"
24 Where some young children spend their time: 2 words
25 Birmingham's state: Abbreviation
27 When Columbus Day is
28 Belonging to us
29 It fits into a lock
32 Water-___ (have fun on a lake)
35 What a private calls a lieutenant, in the army

39 Macadamias and cashews, for example
41 Information, to a computer
42 ___ mail (letters sent to famous people)
43 A vain person may have a big one
44 "You ___ your boots!" ("Absolutely!")
45 Stuck in a ___ (doing the same things over and over)
46 What nodding your head means
48 Permit
49 Ending for "host"

ACROSS

1 Touches softly
5 Practice boxing
9 It's found in a fireplace
12 State next to Nevada
13 "That's terrible!": 2 words
14 Scary sound heard on Halloween
15 Medium ___ (how a steak might be cooked)
16 Not short
17 Metal suit worn by a knight
19 Lacking moisture
21 A man might wear one around his neck
22 Young adult
23 "That's OK ___": 2 words
24 "___ the ramparts we watched ..." (line in "The Star-Spangled Banner")
25 Lunch or dinner, for example
27 Continent that contains Mount Everest
29 ___ Grande (river in Texas)
31 Person, place, or thing
33 Toboggan

36 Part of speech that "quickly" is: Abbreviation
37 It shines in the sky
38 ___ of contents (part of a book)
39 Get an F
41 Villain in "The Lion King"
43 Its capital is Washington, D.C.: Abbreviation
44 "My country, 'tis of ___ ..."
45 Tickle Me ___ (doll)
46 ___ Blanc (the voice of Porky Pig)
47 Just okay: Hyphenated
48 Chair

DOWN

1 Cat's sound
2 One ___ time: 2 words
3 Late to class
4 Mr. Peabody's friend, in cartoons
5 The note after la
6 It might help you remember a family vacation: 2 words

7 "Little Orphan ___"
8 ___ Ebert (famous movie reviewer)
9 As blind as ___: 2 words
10 Stick out like a ___ thumb (be obvious)
11 They might help you remember family vacations: 2 words
18 Half of two
20 "Uh-huh"
23 Pieces of clothing for women
26 Solution: Abbreviation

28 "A mind ___ terrible thing to waste": 2 words
29 People travel down rivers on them
30 Boise's state
32 Aunt's husband
34 "... or ___!" (end of a threat)
35 Hand out the cards
38 Horse's pace
40 Summer sign of the zodiac
42 "Today I ___ man" (what a boy says at his bar mitzvah): 2 words

25

ACROSS

1 Classified ___ (newspaper section)
4 A magician may pull a rabbit out of it
7 How a baby might say "father"
11 Cry from a ghost
12 A conceited person has a large one
13 ___ Trebek (host of "Jeopardy!")
14 Song in "The Lion King": 3 words
17 Big ___ (part of a circus)
18 Insect that makes honey
19 Give permission
22 Hound's hand
23 It cuts wood
26 It turns colors in the autumn
27 "What ___ you say?"
28 One of the Berenstain Bears
29 Search high and ___ (look everywhere)
30 Run for exercise
31 Mike Tyson was a famous one
32 "I'll see what I ___ do"
33 Use scissors

34 Song in "The Lion King": 2 words
40 Puts frosting on a cake
41 ___ cabin (wooden house)
42 Sticky black stuff
43 People write with them
44 Bambi's mother, for example
45 "___ thing leads to another"

DOWN

1 Alphabet beginning
2 "What ___ know?": 2 words
3 In a way: 2 words
4 Give assistance to
5 Grow older
6 "That's a shame": 2 words
7 Chip and ___ (cartoon chipmunks)
8 Name of the prince in the movie "Aladdin"
9 Letters after 1-Down
10 The Tin Woodsman's tool
15 Animal in a dairy

16 Not many
19 "That's ___, folks!"
20 Person who's born in August, probably
21 What a criminal breaks
22 Sloppy eater
23 Lisa Simpson's instrument, for short
24 Relative of a gorilla
25 Opposite of peace
27 Uncle of Huey, Dewey, and Louie
28 Mr. ___ Head (toy)

30 Middle sister on "The Brady Bunch"
31 Last ___ not least
32 Say bad words
33 Place to keep a pet canary
34 Modern and cool
35 Good card in the game blackjack
36 Boyfriend of Barbie
37 Sound from a calf
38 Relax on the beach, maybe
39 "How ___ you doing?"

55

26

ACROSS

1 Buddy
4 Athlete who's in the big leagues
7 ___ Seacrest (host of "American Idol")
11 Manjula's husband, on "The Simpsons"
12 Not him
13 Kind of leather
14 When New Year's Eve is: Abbreviation
15 Like a bump ___ log: 2 words
16 Let
17 Famous male doll
19 Book of fiction
21 Word after "hair" or "life"
23 "___ whillikers!" ("Gosh!")
24 "Birds ___ feather flock together": 2 words
27 Choose
28 Miles ___ hour (what MPH stands for)
29 Someone whose brother or sister has the same birthday
30 Stuff that's left over in a barbecue
31 ___ a ball (enjoys oneself)

32 He had a sidekick named Pokey
33 Secret ___ (spy)
35 From ___ Z: 2 words
36 Christmas song
38 Raggedy ___ (doll)
40 Homophone of "oh"
43 One-___ bandit (nickname for a slot machine)
44 Floor covering
45 Part of a hockey goal
46 The Loch ___ Monster
47 Cars drive on them: Abbreviation
48 Part of a minute: Abbreviation

DOWN

1 Lily ___
2 Baboon's relative
3 Cereal with colorful marshmallows: 2 words
4 Alexander Graham Bell invention
5 Stimpy's friend, in cartoons
6 Some marshmallows in 3-Down: 2 words
7 The Golden ___ ("Do unto others ...")

8 Some marshmallows in
3-Down: 2 words
9 "Much ___ About
Nothing" (play by
William Shakespeare)
10 ___ Mexico
13 Put money in the bank
18 Animal similar to a
moose
20 "___ the fields we go ..."
(line in "Jingle Bells")
21 Health ___ (place where
people try to get in
shape)
22 "___ the season to be
jolly ..."

25 Little white lie
26 "Baa baa black sheep,
have you ___ wool?"
28 You fry bacon in it
29 King ___ (ancient
Egyptian ruler)
31 Hung onto
32 Groups of people
34 Leaves
36 Soup container
37 "You ___ My Sunshine"
(old song)
39 Crazy person
41 ___ Willie Winkie
42 "And so on":
Abbreviation

27

ACROSS

1 Door in a fence
5 "___ no idea!" ("You're kidding!"): 2 words
9 In what way?
12 Location
13 Big brass musical instrument
14 "Who do you think you ___?"
15 Five-pointed shape
16 Tripped
18 TV network that shows news all the time: Abbreviation
20 Note between fa and la
21 ___ Wednesday (religious holiday)
23 Garden of Eden man
27 December 25, for short
30 Yellow-and-black insect
31 Stands a certain way for a sculptor
33 "You ___ me one" ("I'll ask you for a favor back later")
34 The 6 of clubs, for example
36 Despise
37 ___ York City
38 Take a small drink
40 Prefix for "angle" or "cycle"
42 Clark Kent's secret identity

47 Part of a molecule
50 "What's the ___ in trying?" (quitter's question)
51 "I'm so hungry I could ___ horse!": 2 words
52 "___ Lisa" (painting by Leonardo da Vinci)
53 What a baseball player swings
54 Have a short attention ___
55 Animal that's being hunted by another animal

DOWN

1 Fuel for a car
2 You might put it in a frame
3 Special person in a classroom: 2 words
4 Be entitled to
5 "___ up to you"
6 Shack
7 The monkey in "Aladdin"
8 Beavers build them
9 Special person between classrooms: 2 words
10 State that borders the Pacific Ocean: Abbreviation

11 The middle of the school week: Abbreviation

17 What cereal comes in

19 Sleep during the afternoon

21 Start of "The Alphabet Song"

22 Body of water

24 Homer Simpson's exclamation

25 Happy ___ clam: 2 words

26 Was introduced to

28 In ___ of (amazed by)

29 Make stitches

32 ___ on fire (burn)

35 "If I should ___ before I wake ..."

39 The leader of America: Abbreviation

41 A skateboarder might do tricks on it

42 Underwater boat

43 Country that borders Mexico and Canada: Abbreviation

44 Word that can follow "road" or "treasure"

45 ___ distance (far away): 2 words

46 Girl in "The Bobbsey Twins"

48 "___ good turn deserves another"

49 Spring month

28

ACROSS

1 The past tense of "is"
4 Help a broken-down car
7 Strength
12 One of the main TV networks: Abbreviation
13 "Horton Hears a ___!" (Dr. Seuss book)
14 Get rid of chalk marks
15 Family ___ (gathering of family members)
17 Went out with
18 Humongous
19 Cube of hay
20 "That's one small step for ___ ..." (what Neil Armstrong said when he landed on the moon): 2 words
22 It gets delivered almost every day
24 Baseball statistic: Abbreviation
27 ___ and seek
28 Stopping place
29 "This ___ outrage!": 2 words
30 "___ always say ...": 2 words
31 Exclamation from Charlie Brown
32 "The ___ the limit!"
33 Very concerned with one's own looks

35 Prefix that means "one"
36 Metal springs
38 Bring up in conversation
42 Musical that includes the song "Tomorrow"
43 "Where ___?" (lost person's question): 2 words
44 Group that includes the Lakers and the Hawks: Abbreviation
45 Yellow ___ (part of the phone book)
46 Small, crunchy snack
47 ___ rummy

DOWN

1 Card game for two players
2 Nickname of President Lincoln
3 Activity in a lake: 2 words
4 Small branch
5 Exclamation similar to 20-Down
6 Got the prize
7 Move a bicycle
8 Verbal
9 Activity on a lake: Hyphenated
10 Ending for "Siam"

11 Color of a beet
16 Three times three
19 Suggests a price at an auction
20 "I knew it!"
21 Prefix for "interpret" or "spell"
22 Not nice
23 Insect that might go to a picnic
25 Green ___ Packers (pro football team)
26 ___ and outs
29 "Money ___ everything!"
31 Goes up
34 "I cannot tell ___": 2 words
35 An inch is a ___ of length
36 The top of a toothpaste tube
37 Put ___ happy face (smile): 2 words
38 Fellow
39 Big bird from Australia
40 ___-Wan Kenobi ("Star Wars" guy)
41 Girl's name that reads the same forward and backward

29

ACROSS

1 Reaction to poison oak
5 "___ a miracle!"
8 What pigs wallow in
11 Brand of cookie
12 What a movie director yells to end a scene
13 Weak ___ kitten: 2 words
14 Soldier in the comics: 2 words
17 "___ the season ..." (line in "Deck the Halls")
18 "___ got it!"
19 Did some stitching
22 Opposite of wet
23 "He ___ laughs last, laughs best"
26 "___ the Rainbow" (song in "The Wizard of Oz")
27 What the Spanish word "sí" means in English
28 It grows into a plant
29 A fisherman might throw it into the water
30 ___ and far between (rare)
31 Use cash
32 Pen ___ (faraway person you write to)

33 Scooby-___
34 Bald boy in the comics: 2 words
40 Lightning ___
41 "Don't put all your eggs in ___ basket"
42 Group of three singers
43 That lady
44 The Civil ___ (period of American history)
45 Put in the mail

DOWN

1 Steal from
2 "What ___ you driving at?"
3 "___ no evil, hear no evil, speak no evil"
4 Having a higher temperature
5 Frosts
6 "Rub-a-dub-dub, three men in a ___"
7 You might use them instead of an elevator
8 Man
9 "___ your head!" ("Don't be stupid!")
10 April Fools' ___
15 The top of a jar

16 Plant that can grow on walls
19 Prince William, to Prince Charles
20 Christmas ___
21 Moist
22 Mountain ___ (soft drink)
23 Like Willie Winkie
24 The Little Red ___
25 Not even
27 Lemon's color
28 Golf and tennis, for example
30 Opposite of near
31 Go "boo-hoo"
32 You turn it in a book
33 Animal that has fawns
34 Network that shows "Survivor": Abbreviation
35 "I don't understand what you said"
36 ___ trance (hypnotized): 2 words
37 Raw metal
38 Be the champ
39 Wynken, Blynken, and ___ (characters in a rhyme)

30

ACROSS

1 Felt sore
6 Network that shows "ER": Abbreviation
9 Word after "scratch" or "lily"
12 Dinty ___ (brand of stew)
13 ___ of corn
14 Paper that describes a debt
15 Storage room of a house
16 Light rain
18 Unable to hear
20 Show ___ (the world of entertainment)
21 Long ___ (not recently)
23 Not on time
26 One of the Three Bears
29 Things that you toss the rings over when you're playing ringtoss
31 Piglet's mother
32 Moved very quickly
33 "What ___ is new?"
34 Golfers use them
36 This ___ that
37 "Br'er Rabbit and the ___ Baby"
39 It shines in the night sky
41 Sculptors make them

45 Place for bowling
48 Chick's mother
49 Cold cube
50 Hand warmer
51 Finish up
52 "Ready or ___, here I come!"
53 Noisy thing on top of an ambulance

DOWN

1 "I ___ bear of very little brain" (Winnie-the-Pooh quote): 2 words
2 You might put a sleeping bag on it
3 Place to buy some junk food: 3 words
4 Lake that borders Pennsylvania
5 Stick-on design
6 Homer Simpson's next-door neighbor
7 Salad ___
8 A baby might be in one
9 Place to buy some junk food: 2 words
10 Computer service with Buddy Lists and Instant Messages: Abbreviation

11 "Postage ___"
(marking on some
envelopes)
17 Fastens, in a way
19 Speedy
21 King Kong, for one
22 Stuff that can make hair
stay in place
24 Digit on the foot
25 Females who baa
27 Something to write
with
28 Do some math
30 ___ belt (strap in a car)

35 Male deers
38 Wreck
40 "___ Want for Christmas
Is My Two Front Teeth":
2 words
41 That girl
42 The best score for an
Olympic gymnast
43 Prefix that means "the
environment"
44 Part of a tennis match
46 New Year's ___
(December 31)
47 Money used in Japan

31

ACROSS

1 Travel by horse
5 ___ up (support)
9 Dog in the comic strip "Garfield"
10 "Tra ___" (singing sounds): 2 words
11 "In ___ we trust" (phrase found on coins)
14 Foot warmer
15 Odds and ___ (various stuff)
16 Word that can go before "maniac" or "trip"
17 Liquid used in writing
18 Let the cat out of the ___ (tell a secret)
19 Said curse words
21 "And others": Abbreviation
22 Previously owned
24 Metals that have just been dug up
25 Opposite of love
27 Pressed the doorbell
29 Drove faster than the legal limit
31 ___ Cain (actor who played Superman on TV)
33 Silly Putty comes in one
36 Types of things
38 Get ___ of (remove)
39 Spelling ___

40 Break the ___ (start a conversation)
41 Arrive ___ agreement: 2 words
43 Hit the ball softly, in baseball
44 It's up above us
45 Intelligent
46 "Who ___?" (response to a knock at the door): 2 words
47 A watermelon eater might spit it out
48 The son on "The Cosby Show"

DOWN

1 ___ O'Donnell (famous actress and talk-show host)
2 "___ care" ("It doesn't matter to me"): 2 words
3 Vice president starting in 2001: 2 words
4 What someone who saw a mouse might say
5 "___ to meet you" (what you might say when you're introduced to someone)
6 "Home on the ___" (western song)

7 "___ Mother Hubbard went to the cupboard ..."

8 Get a decent grade in a class

11 Vice president starting in 1981: 2 words

12 Shrek, for example

13 "Easy ___ it!" ("Be careful!")

18 Slowly ___ surely

20 Homophone for "one"

23 Disappeared down the hole in a sink

26 Use a plus sign

28 Peanut butter ___ jelly

29 Some winter athletes wear them

30 Make a selection

32 Get chalk marks off a blackboard

34 Magical being who might grant you three wishes

35 "___ the point!" ("Stop wasting time!"): 2 words

37 Carpenters use them for cutting

42 Bow ___ (something a man might wear)

43 ___-O-Honey (candy bar)

32

ACROSS

1 Destroys a balloon
5 Machine where people get money: Abbreviation
8 Wager
11 Heads or ___ (choice during a coin toss)
13 "___ you later, alligator!"
14 Have a debt
15 South American country
17 Sara ___ (brand of frozen desserts)
18 Mother of a fawn
19 Prefix for "pod" or "cycle"
21 What batteries eventually do
24 Moves like a happy dog's tail
27 A chef bakes things in it
30 "___ upon a time ..."
32 New York baseball player
33 Drink that comes from grapes
34 ___ as a bug in a rug
35 Sail the seven ___
37 Find sums
38 How old a person is
40 The ___ of the iceberg

42 Amount at an auction
44 South American country
50 Game that has Wild and Skip cards
51 "___ been thinking ..."
52 Spam, for example: Hyphenated
53 Material used in roadmaking
54 "___ sleeping dogs lie"
55 Territory

DOWN

1 Elementary school group: Abbreviation
2 Homophone of "or"
3 Animal that provides ham
4 You can ride downhill on one
5 "___ recall ...": 2 words
6 Number of cents in a dime
7 Pork or chicken, for example
8 South American country
9 Animal that gives birth to lambs
10 Little wooden thing on a golf course
12 Winter weather

16 The Eagles and the Falcons, for two
20 Move a boat through the water
21 Two, in Spanish
22 Holiday ___ (chain of hotels)
23 South American country
25 "Goodness gracious!"
26 North Carolina or South Dakota, for example
28 Opposite of start
29 Goody-goody on "The Simpsons"

31 It has a shell and a yolk
36 How large something is
39 Badness
41 Wild cat
42 "Everything ___ the kitchen sink"
43 ___ bad mood (upset): 2 words
45 Mother of Cain and Abel
46 A trapeze artist might fall into it
47 You listen with it
48 Little white ___
49 State bordering Georgia: Abbreviation

33

ACROSS

1 Give a darn
5 Right this minute
8 Hit with a laser beam
11 "Once ___ a time ..."
12 Three ___ kind (poker hand): 2 words
13 ___ skating
14 Crispy candy bar
17 The opposite ___ (women, to men)
18 Tommy's father, on "Rugrats"
19 Porky ___
22 Coolio's music
24 Trap
28 Bills that have George Washington on them
30 Magazine that features "Spy vs. Spy"
32 Remain
33 Makes less wild
35 Letters before G
37 On your birthday, this number goes up by one
38 Pen ___ (someone to write to)
40 Animal that has antlers
42 Crispy candy bar: 2 words
48 Flat ___ board: 2 words

49 Long ___ (way back when)
50 See the sights
51 "___ out of here!"
52 Polka ___ (small colorful circle)
53 They live with rams

DOWN

1 Baby bear
2 Hindu character on "The Simpsons"
3 Starts to go moldy
4 Come in
5 Neither here ___ there
6 Goof-___ (lazy people)
7 Hangs around
8 ___ and zag
9 The best card in the game war
10 55 miles ___ hour (common speed limit)
15 Big test
16 Some religious women
19 ___ of gold (what's supposedly at the end of the rainbow)
20 Once ___ while (occasionally): 2 words
21 Valuable stone

23 Scratch ___ (paper to doodle on)

25 "Now playing ___ theater near you!" (movie ad phrase): 2 words

26 Cloth used for dusting

27 Keep an ___ on (watch)

29 Labor Day's month: Abbreviation

31 Fawn, when it grows up

34 Dish of vegetables

36 Instrument you play by blowing into it

39 Company that makes toys you build things with

41 ___-it-all (smarty-pants)

42 Constantly complain

43 Suffix for "Japan"

44 Part of the weekend: Abbreviation

45 A camper might lie down on one

46 ___ cards (things that actors read)

47 60-minute periods: Abbreviation

34

ACROSS

1 It holds a drink
4 "A rolling stone gathers no ___"
8 Trail
12 "So far ___ can tell ...": 2 words
13 Car
14 Pennsylvania city that shares its name with a Great Lake
15 Sound from a ram
16 Musician who plays a brass instrument
18 Slangy way to say no
20 Fish that's hard to catch
21 Mrs. Potts's son, in "Beauty and the Beast"
23 From ___ (completely): 3 words
25 "What ___ care?": 2 words
28 Red flower
29 Child who's a boy
30 Country next to Kuwait
31 "So near and ___ so far"
32 Sneaker, for example
33 Bolts fit into them
34 "Quiet on the ___!" (something a movie director yells)
35 Uncle ___ (man who's a symbol of America)

36 Musician who plays a string instrument
41 Prefix for "guided" or "treat"
44 "___ silly question ...": 2 words
45 China is there
46 Word that can come after "Christmas"
47 Root ___ (drink)
48 You knit with it
49 Deli bread

DOWN

1 It might drive a person from the airport
2 ___ Today (newspaper)
3 Musician who plays a keyboard instrument
4 School course
5 My and your
6 Letters before V
7 "Pick on ___ your own size!"
8 Take the rind off a fruit
9 Paintings and so forth
10 "___ Me Kangaroo Down, Sport" (song)
11 Pronoun for a girl
17 Candy that comes out of a dispenser
19 Big jungle animal

21 "Don't ___ over spilled milk"

22 Tool that's used to dig up weeds

23 A cigarette gets put in it

24 "___ many cooks spoil the broth"

25 Musician who plays a percussion instrument

26 Grain that's sometimes used to feed horses

27 Smart people have high ones: Abbreviation

30 ___ little while (soon): 2 words

32 Body of salt water

34 It might be on top of a Christmas tree

35 Boy on "South Park"

36 Talk a whole lot

37 "___ only as directed" (medicine bottle phrase)

38 Mike and ___ (brand of candy)

39 "This ___ surprise!": 2 words

40 ___ Lancelot (famous knight)

42 Poison ___ (plant you shouldn't touch)

43 "Do you ___ what I mean?"

35

ACROSS

1 What someone in a wheelchair uses instead of stairs
5 Network that showed "The Amazing Race": Abbreviation
8 Simba's uncle, in "The Lion King"
12 Neighborhood
13 Tool used in the garden
14 Deal with
15 Jewels
16 Bird that flies at night
17 "Jeopardy!" host Trebek
18 Bart Simpson's bus driver
20 Little ___ (girl from comic books)
22 Mink coat, for example
24 The ___ Enterprise (spaceship on "Star Trek")
26 Sour fruit
29 "Do ___ say!": 2 words
30 Opposite of most
32 "___ the Builder"
33 Looks through a book
35 Pay-___-view
36 Put ___ fight: 2 words
37 It's attached to a tree branch
39 Catches

41 Comes up with a total
43 Free ___ bird: 2 words
45 Cain and Abel's father
48 Make very wet
49 Animal that says "meow"
50 "Fa ___" (sounds in a song): 2 words
51 Door openers
52 Where the retina and pupil are
53 Changed the color of

DOWN

1 Old cloth
2 "How ___ you?"
3 It's observed in May: 2 words
4 Not the present or future
5 Decide
6 An arrow is shot out of one
7 Buy and ___
8 What you weigh things on
9 It's observed in October: 2 words
10 Relative of a chimpanzee

74

11 Tyrannosaurus ___
19 City in Oklahoma
21 Prefix for "violet"
22 Distant
23 Put to good ___ (take advantage of)
25 Sticky stuff in a tree
27 Alley-___ (basketball move)
28 The New York Knicks are in it: Abbreviation
31 One of the houses of Congress

34 Teachers sit behind them
38 ___ card (jack, queen, or king)
40 Having no hair
41 "Go ___ your mother"
42 Homophone of "dough"
44 "You don't ___!" ("No kidding!")
46 Ginger ___
47 Magazine that's a rival of Cracked

36

ACROSS

1 Pellets in toy guns
4 "Happy" is this kind of word: Abbreviation
7 Month after February: Abbreviation
10 Like a fish ___ of water
11 Some people born in the summer
13 Single showing of a TV show
15 Felt sore all over
17 Shade of color
18 Join with stitches
20 Joint in the leg
21 Someone with a halo
23 The hard thing in the center of a peach
25 Letters after K
26 "___ sesame!" (what Ali Baba said)
28 Short letter
30 Stomach muscles, for short
32 Gooey stuff on a road
34 Desi ___ (actor on "I Love Lucy")
37 Connect the ___ (simple puzzle)
39 ___ on the back (kind of encouragement)
41 Not twice
42 Mr. ___ (Fred Flintstone's boss)
44 They heal the sick
46 What hospital food is served on
47 "What did ___ wrong?": 2 words
48 What you hit a badminton birdie over
49 Dark-colored bread
50 A little strange

DOWN

1 "___, hiss!" (sounds for the villain)
2 They bloom into flowers
3 Hard to climb
4 Southern U.S. state: Abbreviation
5 Stack of cards
6 One of the Beatles: 2 words
7 "... I ___ man with seven wives": 2 words
8 Neat as ___: 2 words
9 One of the Beatles: 2 words
12 "Things are not always what they ___"

14 A ___ in the right direction

16 Room where you might watch TV

19 No-___ situation (case where nothing can go right)

22 Live and ___ live (don't interfere in what other people do)

24 Come ___ decision: 2 words

27 Short sleep

29 Pace for a horse

30 They sell things

31 Connecting device that gets put through a nut

33 A car's dashboard usually has one

35 Unit of measure for land

36 Liveliness

38 "___ in touch!"

40 One of Ned Flanders's kids, on "The Simpsons"

43 Bud on a potato

45 Food fish

37

ACROSS

1 Mother on "The Brady Bunch"
6 Apply gently, like makeup
9 Stadium
10 Ram's mate, on a farm
11 Drink through a straw
14 You can make knots in them
15 Girl Scout level between Junior and Senior
17 Famous ___ (brand of cookies)
18 ___ attention (listen carefully)
19 Place
20 It's used to pave streets
21 ___ grace (recite a prayer before eating)
22 Small units of weight
23 Not fat
25 Prefix for "series" or "van"
26 Butter ___ (ice cream flavor)
28 Obi-___ Kenobi ("Star Wars" character)
29 "I ___ the picture" ("I understand")
32 Egg's shape

33 On ___ of the world (very happy)
34 Old-fashioned way to say "you"
35 Act
37 "The Hunchback of ___ Dame" (Disney movie)
38 Go off the deep ___ (go crazy)
39 Give credit where credit is ___
40 One more time
41 Home for lions
42 Gets in place for a photo

DOWN

1 Unit of weight for jewels
2 Smell
3 It shows your grades: 2 words
4 What you get when you ask for change for a five-dollar bill
5 ___ Vegas
6 Tooth ___ (problem for a dentist)
7 "___ in a Manger" (Christmas carol)

8 Get up on the wrong side of the ___

11 What a good student gets on a 3-Down: 2 words

12 Object

13 Black-eyed ___

16 Deserve

18 You need it for frying

21 "It's a ___ to tell a lie"

22 ___ rummy (card game)

24 50%

25 A tourist might follow one

26 The head of the Catholic church

27 Like the numbers 2, 4, and 6

28 Females

30 Spine-tingling

31 High-school students

33 ___-false test

34 How you might order fast food: 2 words

36 Opposite of 27-Down

37 Catch forty winks

38

ACROSS

1 "___ crying out loud!"
4 "___ you say something?"
7 State in New England
12 One, in Spanish
13 Path followed by a mail carrier: Abbreviation
14 Material that's used to make pueblos in the southwestern U.S.
15 Word after "sting" or "X"
16 Looney Tunes animal: 2 words
18 ___ conditioner
20 ___ Angeles
21 Looney Tunes animal
25 ___ and hers
28 ___ Sampras (tennis player)
29 Letters on small batteries
30 Piggy ___ (place to save money)
31 "Are there ___ questions?"
32 Looney Tunes animal: 2 words
34 Friend of Grumpy and Happy

35 Peculiar
36 Looney Tunes animal: 3 words
41 Where Santa invites kids to sit
44 Important happening
45 Bird that eats mice
46 Private ___ (sleuth)
47 Campers stay in them
48 ___ Moines
49 Homophone for "see"

DOWN

1 It's on a dog's skin
2 Put ___ show (entertain people): 2 words
3 Kings and queens, for example
4 Rapper who discovered Eminem: 2 words, abbreviation
5 "Give ___ try!": 2 words
6 Letters after C
7 Leader of the city
8 Does some arithmetic
9 Evidence of a debt
10 "Will & Grace" network: Abbreviation
11 Frightened sound

17 Insects that bother dogs

19 "___ Been Working on the Railroad"

21 Health ___ (place where people go to get fit)

22 Japanese money

23 Soy ___

24 Price ___

25 What you hold suitcases by

26 Hotel

27 Where the sun and moon are

30 Flower that hasn't bloomed yet

32 Metal fastenings

33 You eat cereal out of them

34 Damage a car's bumper

36 House animal

37 New Year's ___

38 It needs ink

39 What 43-Down comes in

40 Farm female

42 Yes, in the military

43 Small round vegetable

39

ACROSS

1 Pole on a ship
5 Little ___ (tiny amount)
8 Health resorts
12 Disappear ___ thin air
13 High card in many games
14 Keep ___ (go on): 2 words
15 Dish that contains meat and vegetables
16 Precious stone
17 Extremely
18 "The early bird ___ the worm"
20 Where ships come in
22 Really love
24 One more than nine
25 "I ___ you one"
28 Letters used in an emergency
29 Nut that comes from an oak tree
31 "Don't quit your ___ job"
32 One step ___ time: 2 words
33 Speak
34 Wipe out

36 ___ one's head (thinks)
38 Bric-a-___ (various stuff)
39 Mean monster
41 Shoot ___ breeze (chat)
43 "Leave ___ me": 2 words
46 Part of speech
47 Be untruthful
48 Changed the color of one's hair
49 Direction on a compass
50 It means "most" at the end of a word
51 It might be pulled by a team of dogs

DOWN

1 Prefix for "behave"
2 Little pest
3 Prehistoric animal
4 The Leaning ___ of Pisa
5 What groceries are put into
6 Cubes of frozen water
7 Lose your ___ (have a fit)
8 Rescue
9 Prehistoric animal
10 People need it to live

11 Where a pig might live
19 Poke fun at
21 Opposite of outer
22 Sharp ___ tack: 2 words
23 Wakko and Yakko's sister, on "Animaniacs"
24 Something to play with
26 "It ___ a dark and stormy night"
27 Organ of sight
30 Where a king might live

35 Sudden military attacks
37 Mailed
38 Red vegetable
39 Number said right before "liftoff!"
40 ___ long way (endure): 2 words
42 That man's
44 Peg used by Tiger Woods
45 Even's opposite

40

ACROSS

1 Suggest a price
4 Uses a shovel
8 Word on a light switch
11 "Do ___ tell you!":
2 words
12 In any amount: 2 words
14 Character on "Rugrats"
15 ___ Vegas (Nevada city)
16 Woman on "Sesame Street"
17 Feeling of fear
19 Police officer
21 Things that attempt to sell products
22 Take a ___ (stop standing)
23 Was a passenger
24 ___ down to business
25 Mother
27 A single time
29 "___ Yankee Doodle Dandy": 2 words
31 Frankenstein's assistant
33 ___ up (completely finishes)
36 Word that goes with "neither"
37 Chicken drumstick
38 Digging tool

39 Having no clothes on
41 Took part in a footrace
43 Bruce ___ (star of martial arts movies)
44 The first host of "Blue's Clues"
45 A conceited person has a big one
46 The last part
47 Beef ___ (hearty meal)
48 Fix a torn piece of clothing

DOWN

1 ___ eagle (American bird)
2 "This ___ stickup!":
2 words
3 Music that was popular in the 1970s
4 Make wet
5 "Give ___ shot!":
2 words
6 Place to buy used items:
2 words
7 Thing on a playground
8 ___ and ends (various items)

84

9 "Out of the frying pan, into the ___"

10 Place to buy used items: 2 words

13 Final

18 One ___ time (not as a group): 2 words

20 Unpleasant smell

23 Fury

26 Kind of fungus

28 You drink out of it

29 Hotels

30 Defenses around castles

32 Villains in many fairy tales

34 Garden of ___ (place in the Bible)

35 Item planted in a garden

38 What igloos are made of

40 The night before a holiday

42 Number of years you've been alive

ANSWERS

1

```
E L S E   O H O   A R T
L E I A   I N A N   L E O
F I R S T N A M E   A X E
      T O S   S U B
A P E   W I N S   S A F E
S E C O N D B A S E M E N
H A U L   E C H O   A D D
      A D S   A L A
M A D   T H I R D R A T E
A G O   E A T A   C R A B
P E R   M T S   H E R B
```

2

```
A B C   L A S H   S I P S
S E A   I N T O   A S I A
A D V E N T U R E L A N D
      E V E S   R A T
T I M I D   P O T   F E D
O V A L   B A R   C O L E
P E N   H O W   G E R M S
      K I T   P U N T
M A I N S T R E E T U S A
A B L E   L A P S   N A P
T E L E   E Y E S   E W E
```

3

```
S A M   L E D   A S I A
A P E   A X E   W I N S
P U M P K I N P A T C H
    B E E T   O K S
D I E T S   B E E   C O W
A C R E   H I T   C O L A
Y E S   B E G   L A N D S
      A I R   M I S T
J A C K O L A N T E R N
I S E E   O N E   S U E
M A S S   T E N   T N T
```

4

```
L A S E R   N B C   E E L
A P P L E   O U R   I V E
B E A M S   S N I F F E D
      C O T S   S E L F
T H E   S E W   S E E D S
W I N D   T E N   A L O T
O P E R A   B U S   T O Y
      E A R S   T A C O
G A D G E T S   T O W E L
A L L   N A P   A R E N A
P I E   T R Y   N E R D Y
```

5

```
A D S   D I S H   I S I T
P A W   I D E A   R A C E
E Y E B R O W S   A M E N
      D O T   A N T
O H I O   W A R N   H I P
L O S   C A R E D   E V E
D O H   A G E D   P E E P
      C P R   T E A
H A H A   T R I A N G L E
U S E S   O I N K   L A W
G I F T   N O N E   E S E
```

6

```
L I P   C O P   P A W N S
A C T   A R E   A R I E L
B E A N B A G   W E N D Y
      I L L   H E A D
E A G L E   S A D   B E E
A C R E   T O Y   W A V E
T E A   C O B   B A G E L
      B L O W   P A N
A L B U M   H A N D B A G
W E A R E   E G G   U S E
E D G E S   Y E S   S A T
```

7

B	A	S	E		M	E	S	A		T	E	A
A	R	T	S		A	X	E	S		H	A	M
T	R	E	E		M	I	L	K		E	V	E
H	O	T		D	A	T	E		W	R	E	N
	W	H	O	A		S	C	R	A	M	S	
		O	N	T	O		T	A	C	O		
	E	S	C	A	P	E		N	O	M	E	
P	A	C	E		E	A	S	T		E	L	M
A	G	O		I	N	T	O		O	T	T	O
P	E	P		N	E	M	O		N	E	O	N
A	R	E		E	D	E	N		O	R	N	O

8

P	R	O	S		B	A	G	S				
T	A	R	P		A	B	L	E		F	E	E
A	D	A	Y		B	E	A	T		R	A	Y
S	I	N		Y	E	A	R		L	U	R	E
	O	G	R	E		R	E	T	A	I	N	
		E	A	T	S		S	E	N	T		
	A	S	K	I	N	G		L	A	P	S	
O	B	O	E		O	R	A	L		U	N	O
F	E	D		I	R	A	N		S	N	A	P
A	L	A		T	E	N	T		A	C	R	E
				A	R	T	S		T	H	E	N

9

M	A	T	T		A	D	A	M		D	I	G
A	C	O	W		L	O	N	E		I	N	N
M	A	G	I	C	I	A	N	S		N	B	A
A	R	E	N	A			S	W	E	E	T	
S	E	T		N	A	S	A		A	D	D	S
			W	I	T	C	H	E	S			
S	H	O	E		M	I	S	T		S	P	A
P	A	N	D	A			T	A	C	O	S	
A	S	I		S	O	R	C	E	R	E	R	S
I	T	O		A	R	E	A		A	N	T	E
N	O	N		N	E	X	T		B	E	S	T

10

S	A	T	A	N		O	C	T		A	H	A
A	L	I	C	E		W	A	R		T	O	N
N	A	S	H	V	I	L	L	E		L	E	D
			E	E	L		M	A	M	A		
T	I	L		R	A	N		T	E	N	T	S
E	D	I	T		Y	E	T		A	T	O	P
N	O	N	O	S		W	E	B		A	M	Y
		C	O	O	L		R	O	D			
F	A	O		D	E	S	M	O	I	N	E	S
I	L	L		A	G	E		S	C	E	N	T
B	E	N		S	O	X		T	E	D	D	Y

11

S	U	I	T		W	A	S		B	A	T	H
O	N	T	O		A	B	E		A	S	I	A
B	O	S	T	O	N	C	E	L	T	I	C	S
			O	U	T		D	A	M			
B	A	R		R	E	D		W	A	G	O	N
I	R	A	Q		D	O	T		N	O	N	E
G	E	T	U	P		A	I	R		D	A	D
			A	R	T		C	A	L			
N	E	W	Y	O	R	K	K	N	I	C	K	S
E	V	I	L		E	E	L		S	A	I	L
G	E	N	E		E	Y	E		A	N	D	Y

12

				T	O	P	S		A	M	I	
H	I	J		I	D	E	A		L	I	S	T
U	S	A		C	O	P	Y		I	S	S	O
L	A	C	E		R	E	A	D		S	U	E
A	N	K	L	E	S		H	E	M	M	E	D
		H	E	X			L	O	U			
C	H	O	M	P	S		S	I	N	F	U	L
O	E	R		O	U	C	H		A	F	R	O
S	A	N	K		G	O	R	E		E	G	O
T	R	E	E		A	P	E	S		T	E	N
	T	R	Y		R	E	D	S				

13

```
AMMO  POST  LOW
BEAR  AUTO  INA
CAPEDCRUSADER
   OAK  NAP
HAS MEN  YEAST
ITIS DEF  SHOE
TEXAS TRA AXE
   ITS ALA
THEDYNAMICDUO
WAY LOVE  TINA
OWE EWES  SPOT
```

14

```
HARES DIP  AHA
ADULT USA  SIS
MESSY ENGLISH
   SELL TEE
ALI EAR  STIRS
BEAM BIZ  STOP
CONES DOC ATA
   ALA ORAL
SPANISH EXITS
ART PIE  PLANT
TOM SAY  TENTS
```

15

```
   NASA  ABCD
CAP APAR  DARE
ASI GERM  STEW
LICK MAYO TEE
LATIFAH MILKY
  IRON  FIRE
SMOKE ARTISTS
NAN SILO  SHOO
ORAL SIZE INA
WIRE EVER PER
YOYO EENY
```

16

```
GABS  TOSS
ABEE INTO  CAT
MELT MEAN  AIR
EEL TEST  ANDY
 TYPES EARNS
 FAR   LEO
CLIMB  SLANG
DOOR ACTS  BEN
IMP ACHE  CANE
DES SOAP  ALIE
 ANTS  BLED
```

17

```
DEC ALVA  AMAN
AAH LEIS  CAPE
TRI LOOP  TYPE
ENEMY LIP  OLD
SAFE RARE  REY
 WAVE  IRAQ
ALI AMEN  SUBS
LAG NOR  CHILI
TUGS VASE  MEG
ARUT ESPN  BEN
RAMS SEAT  YDS
```

18

```
MEG PAIN  OPEN
AGE ONTO  TREE
COMPUTER  TILT
  ARE  SON
ARMY NOTE  TIP
BOO INDIA  EVE
CON MADE  AREA
 ISA  DIG
LATE KEYBOARD
ALOT ISEE  BYE
WARS TEST  SEW
```

19

```
PART SCAM FEW
ASIA COLA AYE
WIMBLEDON RED
     SUN TEAM
SHE AIS  PEAR
KENTUCKYDERBY
INTO YOO  SEE
  RAIN DOA
AMI SUPERBOWL
DOE IDOL AREA
SOS NEWS TEES
```

20

```
MUD TOAD LOIS
ASA EASE ANDA
PEG DRIFTWOOD
   WEDS ERN
AGONY DAY RAN
HOOD NOT ZERO
ADD MOE CODED
   EAR MEOW
HOLLYWOOD OFF
IRIS ANNA  OIL
PETE YEAR  DRY
```

21

```
BAT DEW VOTES
ALI INA AGREE
ALMONDS DRAKE
  EVES BEEN
ARMED HER  SHE
ROAR BIT APES
ETC GAS FRONT
  HOUR PEER
ALIVE PINATAS
NINES INC  EGO
TEENS GEE  ROW
```

22

```
LOSS OAR CHAP
AUTO PIE LISA
STUFFEDANIMAL
   TIN SIP
RIVET POP FOR
OVEN TEN CONE
WET ZAP BLEED
   TON LEO
ACTIONFIGURES
NAIL ELM DONE
TREE DYE YODA
```

23

```
DEJA FACT BOW
ASAN UTAH ONA
DENT NOVEMBER
  USE EYE
USA ADAM TOOK
PER TALES CUE
SAYS YANK TRY
  INC IDO
FEBRUARY ABLE
AGE TRUE TEES
NOT SETS ARTS
```

24

```
     PATS SPAR
ASH UTAH OHNO
BOO RARE LONG
ARMOR DRY TIE
TEEN BYME OER
  MEAL ASIA
RIO NOUN SLED
ADV SUN TABLE
FAIL SCAR USA
THEE ELMO MEL
SOSO SEAT
```

25

```
A D S   H A T   D A D A
B O O   E G O   A L E X
C I R C L E O F L I F E
    T O P   B E E
A L L O W   P A W   S A W
L E A F   D I D   P A P A
L O W   J O G   B O X E R
    C A N   C U T
H A K U N A M A T A T A
I C E S   L O G   T A R
P E N S   D O E   O N E
```

26

```
P A L   P R O   R Y A N
A P U   H E R   S U E D E
D E C   O N A   A L L O W
    K E N   N O V E L
S T Y L E   G E E   O F A
P I C K   P E R   T W I N
A S H   H A S   G U M B Y
    A G E N T   A T O
C A R O L   A N N   O W E
A R M E D   R U G   N E T
N E S S   S T S   S E C
```

27

```
G A T E   I H A D   H O W
A R E A   T U B A   A R E
S T A R   S T U M B L E D
    C N N   S O L
A S H   A D A M   X M A S
B E E   P O S E S   O W E
C A R D   H A T E   N E W
    S I P   T R I
S U P E R M A N   A T O M
U S E   E A T A   M O N A
B A T   S P A N   P R E Y
```

28

```
W A S   T O W   P O W E R
A B C   W H O   E R A S E
R E U N I O N   D A T E D
    B I G   B A L E
A M A N   M A I L   R B I
H I D E   E N D   I S A N
A S I   R A T S   S K Y S
    V A I N   U N I
C O I L S   M E N T I O N
A N N I E   A M I   N B A
P A G E S   N U T   G I N
```

29

```
R A S H   I T S   M U D
O R E O   C U T   A S A
B E E T L E B A I L E Y
    T I S   I V E
S E W E D   D R Y   W H O
O V E R   Y E S   S E E D
N E T   F E W   S P E N D
    P A L   D O O
C H A R L I E B R O W N
B U G   O N E   T R I O
S H E   W A R   S E N D
```

30

```
A C H E D   N B C   P A D
M O O R E   E A R   I O U
A T T I C   D R I Z Z L E
    D E A F   B I Z
A G O   L A T E   P A P A
P E G S   S O W   S P E D
E L S E   T E E S   A N D
    T A R   S T A R
S T A T U E S   A L L E Y
H E N   I C E   G L O V E
E N D   N O T   S I R E N
```

91

31

```
RIDE  PROP
ODIE  LALA  GOD
SOCK  ENDS  EGO
INK  BAG  SWORE
ETC  USED  ORES
    HATE  RANG
SPED  DEAN  EGG
KINDS  RID  BEE
ICE  ATAN  BUNT
SKY  WISE  ISIT
    SEED  THEO
```

32

```
POPS  ATM  BET
TAILS  SEE  OWE
ARGENTINA  LEE
    DOE  TRI
DIE  WAGS  OVEN
ONCE  MET  WINE
SNUG  SEAS  ADD
    AGE  TIP
BID  VENEZUELA
UNO  IVE  EMAIL
TAR  LET  AREA
```

33

```
CARE  NOW  ZAP
UPON  OFA  ICE
BUTTERFINGER
    SEX  STU
PIG  RAP  SNARE
ONES  MAD  STAY
TAMES  DEF  AGE
    PAL  ELK
NESTLECRUNCH
ASA  AGO  TOUR
GET  DOT  EWES
```

34

```
CUP  MOSS  PATH
ASI  AUTO  ERIE
BAA  TRUMPETER
    NAH  EEL
CHIP  ATOZ  DOI
ROSE  SON  IRAQ
YET  SHOE  NUTS
    SET  SAM
GUITARIST  MIS
ASKA  ASIA  EVE
BEER  YARN  RYE
```

35

```
RAMP  CBS  SCAR
AREA  HOE  COPE
GEMS  OWL  ALEX
    OTTO  LULU
FUR  USS  LEMON
ASI  LEAST  BOB
READS  PER  UPA
    LEAF  NABS
ADDS  ASA  ADAM
SOAK  CAT  LALA
KEYS  EYE  DYED
```

36

```
    BBS  ADJ
MAR  OUT  LEOS
EPISODE  ACHED
TINT  SEW  KNEE
ANGEL  PIT  LMN
  OPEN  NOTE
ABS  TAR  ARNAZ
DOTS  PAT  ONCE
SLATE  DOCTORS
  TRAY  IDO  NET
  RYE  ODD
```

37

```
C A R O L   D A B   ▓
A R E N A   E W E   S I P
R O P E S   C A D E T T E
A M O S   P A Y   A R E A
T A R   S A Y   G R A M S
▓   T H I N   M I N I   ▓
P E C A N   W A N   G E T
O V A L   T O P   T H E E
P E R F O R M   N O T R E
E N D   D U E   A G A I N
▓   D E N   P O S E S
```

38

```
F O R   D I D   M A I N E
U N O   R T E   A D O B E
R A Y   D A F F Y D U C K
▓ A I R   L O S ▓
S Y L V E S T E R   H I S
P E T E   A A A   B A N K
A N Y   B U G S B U N N Y
▓ D O C   O D D ▓
P E P E L E P E W   L A P
E V E N T   O W L   E Y E
T E N T S   D E S   S E A
```

39

```
M A S T   B I T   S P A S
I N T O   A C E   A T I T
S T E W   G E M   V E R Y
▓ G E T S   P I E R
A D O R E   T E N   O W E
S O S   A C O R N   D A Y
A T A   S A Y   E R A S E
▓ U S E S   B R A C ▓
O G R E   T H E   I T T O
N O U N   L I E   D Y E D
E A S T   E S T   S L E D
```

40

```
▓ B I D   D I G S ▓
O F F   A S I   A T A L L
D I L   L A S   M A R I A
D R E A D   C O P   A D S
S E A T   R O D E   G E T
▓ M A M A   O N C E ▓
I M A   I G O R   U S E S
N O R   L E G   S P A D E
N A K E D   R A N   L E E
S T E V E   E G O   E N D
▓ S T E W   S E W ▓
```

ABOUT THE AUTHOR

Trip Payne is a professional puzzlemaker living in Fort Lauderdale, Florida. He made his first puzzles when he was in elementary school, had his first puzzle in a national magazine when he was in junior high, and worked for a major puzzle magazine when he was in college. He has won the American Crossword Puzzle Tournament three times.

He has made kids' puzzles for such places as *Scholastic News*, *Games Junior*, and *TV Guide*. This is his sixth book in the "Crosswords for Kids" series for Sterling Publishing.

Dan Wenke at Bern-Art Studios

WHAT IS MENSA?

Mensa
The High IQ Society

Mensa is the international society for people with a high IQ. We have more than 100,000 members in over 40 countries worldwide.

The society's aims are:
- to identify and foster human intelligence for the benefit of humanity;
- to encourage research in the nature, characteristics, and uses of intelligence;
- to provide a stimulating intellectual and social environment for its members.

Anyone with an IQ score in the top two percent of population is eligible to become a member of Mensa—are you the "one in 50" we've been looking for?

Mensa membership offers an excellent range of benefits:
- Networking and social activities nationally and around the world;
- Special Interest Groups (hundreds of chances to pursue your hobbies and interests—from art to zoology!);
- Monthly International Journal, national magazines, and regional newsletters;

- Local meetings—from game challenges to food and drink;
- National and international weekend gatherings and conferences;
- Intellectually stimulating lectures and seminars;
- Access to the worldwide SIGHT network for travelers and hosts.

For more information about Mensa International:
www.mensa.org
Mensa International
15 The Ivories
6–8 Northampton Street
Islington, London N1 2HY
United Kingdom

For more information about American Mensa:
www.us.mensa.org
Telephone: (817) 607-0060
American Mensa Ltd.
1229 Corporate Drive West
Arlington, TX 76006-6103 USA

For more information about British Mensa
(UK and Ireland):
www.mensa.org.uk
Telephone: +44 (0) 1902 772771
E-mail: enquiries@mensa.org.uk
British Mensa Ltd.
St. John's House
St. John's Square
Wolverhampton WV2 4AH
United Kingdom